GS LOOK

HARPER & ROW , PUBLISHERS

NEW YORK · CAMBRIDGE · PHILADELPHIA · SAN FRANCISCO · WASHINGTON · LONDON · MEXICO CITY · SAO PAULO · SINGAPORE · SYDNEY

FIRST EDITION

Designer: Frank Olinsky

Copyeditor: John R. Simon

Library of Congress Cataloging-in-Publication Data

Talking Heads.
    What the songs look like.

    Includes index.
    1. New wave music—United States—Texts. I. Olinsky, Frank. II. Talking Heads (Musical group). III. Title.
ML54.6.B9504 1987   784.5′405   86-46338
ISBN 0-06-055117-8   87 88 89 90 91 SCP 10 9 8 7 6 5 4 3 2 1
ISBN 0-06-096205-4 (pbk.) 87 88 89 90 91 SCP 10 9 8 7 6 5 4 3 2 1

CONTENTS

PREFACE

by FRANK OLINSKY

I came up with the idea for an illustrated Talking Heads book in 1983, having always been a fan of Talking Heads and considering their words and music to be combined in a way unparalleled since the Beatles (one inspiration for this book was Alan Aldridge's *The Beatles' Illustrated Lyrics* which came out in 1969).

With the assistance of some of my illustrator and photographer friends (Iris Brown, Deborah Feingold, Stephen Guarnaccia, Stephen Kroninger, Mark Marek, Sara Schwartz, Kurt Vargo and Stewart Wilson: for various reasons some of their original work never made it into this book, but I am still indebted to them) I prepared some sample page layouts, and wrote to Talking Head's management describing my concept as simply as possible and expecting nothing. The response was enthusiastic and immediate. Their office arranged for a meeting, and the idea really struck. A call was made to David Byrne while I was there and the work was sent to his home. (It seems his girlfriend particularly liked a drawing I had done of David. She said I made him look like Little Lulu).

On my first visit, David greeted me at the door and we went upstairs and immediately began a sort of show-and-tell with each other. He went over my stuff, told me about artists he liked and showed me some of his own artwork. He said he liked the idea as long as it would be an art book

and not a rock-and-roll fan book, not lots of band pictures.

We came up with lists of potential artists—a mixture of known and little known fine artists, illustrators and photographers—an eclectic group. David thought the artists should use the lyrics as jumping-off places, with the work not having to have any literal references to the songs. I wanted as much original work as possible; art created especially for this book. Otherwise I tried to get pieces that hadn't been widely seen and were matched to a particular song lyric. I contacted artists from all over the world. Some were David's acquaintances. Some were my "art heroes" whom I had long admired. Almost everyone was enthusiastic and more than willing to contribute something.

I wanted the lyrics to read like newspaper stories or magazine articles so I had them set in justified columns to shed new light on familiar material.

When the artwork arrived, I looked at everything for a long time and began to notice certain images, colors and themes which connected pieces together: visual episodes, gestures, faces, furniture, cars and all sorts of things—all the "stuff" of David's songs. These various small episodes were arranged into a larger visual narrative which ran from the obvious to the oblique. Somehow it began to make a "sense" of its own, another dimension which was totally unplanned.

INTRODUCTION

by DAVID BYRNE

When you sing words, they have a completely different meaning than when you read them.

When somebody yells "Fire!" it's really different than seeing that word written on a piece of paper.

When the government or a corporation uses a picture, a specific meaning is intended. What are these pictures selling?

If you knew an atomic war had broken out and you had at the most a half-hour to live, what would you choose to look at?

If you were putting a personal ad in the paper and couldn't use a picture of yourself, what image would you use?

When I moved to New York about 1974, I was writing some songs, sort of dabbling . . . playing a little bit of music to myself; I never thought I'd make a living at it. Most of my time was spent working out ideas for what I called the "Nielson Rating System for the Arts," the idea being to develop a system that would open up lines of communication between viewers and visual artists. It would work in two ways—the viewer would find out what sort of things were out there that affected and moved him or her . . . and the artists, in turn, could find out who they were talking to. If an artist would rather talk to someone else, then he or she could find out what that someone was interested in—and what kind of visual language to speak.

The whole system involved a lot of computer terminals, cross-referencing, answering multiple choice and yes/no questions, and checking true/false statements. Then, all of that information would go into a giant computer that everyone had access to, artists and viewers alike. This random sample of people would be asked questions like: What did they think visual art was for? . . . Why did they like straight lines better than squiggly lines? . . . Would they just as soon watch stuff on television? . . . Did they like art better in books or in museums? . . . Was making something ugly a way of making it romantic? . . . and so on.

In the back of my mind, I must have known that this whole system was kind of stupid and unworkable on the practical level, but on another level it did raise some interesting questions. For instance, are visual artists really interested in what the audience thinks? Do artists really believe that they are the antennae of society? Does the audience believe that? Does the audience hope the artists believe that?

The assumption behind this proposed system is that visual art has a practical and real value, that even decoration is not meaningless, and that somehow, through all this question asking and answering, the real value of this stuff to people's lives might emerge—art would turn into a product, a commodity in a kind of Marxist sense, as opposed to the current popular viewpoint in which art is valued as a rare one-of-a-kind jewel or as a religious icon, a unique expression of a savage soul. My assumption at the time was that one result of this system might be that art production would increase, and at the same time prices would drop. The visual artist might, in the course of using a system like this over a number of years, reach a wider and wider audience and do so without diluting the content or depth of his or her work.

A "functional but not craftlike" way of treating visual art might return folks to an attitude that existed in the very early part of the European medieval period—and still exists in much of the world—where such a heavy value is not placed on the individual experience. Sometimes there seems to be evidence of a slight return to this way of thinking, which might actually be a good thing . . . it might be the only way that a lot of people can live together.

Some of the people whose work appears in this book probably listen to records or to the radio while they work. A lot of people listen to music while they work. I tried to write lyrics and watch television once at the same time, hoping they would kind of fuse together. It didn't work very well. Watching television is not like going to the beach.

A lot of people were not included in this book, and maybe the ones represented here feel they have nothing in common with the other people whose work is included. Had I written a *lot* more songs, more people could have been invited and this could have been a thicker book. That's true.

Imagine your daily paper will soon be the size of a phonebook . . . that seems to be the direction we're going in. If these pictures are news, then the words can be thought of as captions, or, if the words are news, then the pictures are the hard evidence.

What are these pictures selling? They're not selling records.

San Francisco, 1986

THINGS TO DO

1. Try to (walking quickly) be
2. Count to ten, smile, count to ten
3. Big shoes
4. Watching big shoes
5. Buying things and spending money
6. Counting things
7. Inventing facial expressions
8. Parking
9. Fixing things
10. Writing letters
11. Studying maps, inventing street names
12. Scraping the garden
13. Putting the garden in the house
14. Pointy things
15. Bumpy things
16. Broken things
17. Finding the bank
18. Finding the window
19. Writing a book
20. Finding the book
21. Little houses
22. Counting the houses
23. Drinking things
24. Watching other things
25. Putting houses next to bumpy things
26. Shaking things next to other things

MEMORIES CAN'T WAIT

Do you remember anyone here? No, you don't remember anything at all. I'm sleeping, I'm flat on my back. Never woke up, had no regrets.

There's a party in my mind and it never stops. There's a party up there all the time, they'll party till they drop.

Other people can go home . . . other people, they can split. I'll be here all the time . . . I can never quit.

Take a walk through the land of shadows. Take a walk through the peaceful meadows. Try not to look so disappointed. It isn't what you hoped for, is it?

There's a party in my mind, and I hope it never stops. I'm stuck here in this seat . . . I might not stand up.

Other people can go home . . . everybody else will split. I'll be here all the time . . . I can never quit.

Everything is very quiet. Everyone has gone to sleep. I'm wide awake on memories. These memories can't wait.

THIS MUST BE THE PLACE (Naive Melody)

Home is where I want to be. Pick me up and turn me 'round. I feel numb, born with a weak heart. So I guess I must be having fun. The less we say about it the better. Make it up as we go along. Feet on the ground, head in the sky. It's OK, I know nothing's wrong.

I got plenty of time. You got light in your eyes. And you're standing here beside me, I love the passing of time. Never for money, always for love. Cover up and say goodnight.

Home is where I want to be, but I guess I'm already there. I come home, she lifted up her wings, guess that this must be the place. I can't tell one from another, did I find you, or you find me? There was a time before we were born, if someone asks, this is where I'll be.

We drift in and out. Sing into my mouth. Out of all those kinds of people, you got a face with a view. I'm just an animal looking for a home. Share the same space for a minute or two. And you love me till my heart stops, love me till I'm dead. Eyes that light up, eyes look through you. Cover up the blank spots, hit me on the head.

CROSSEYED AND PAINLESS

WORDS BY DAVID BYRNE
AND BRIAN ENO

Lost my shape trying to act casual. Can't stop, I might end up in the hospital. I'm changing my shape, I feel like an accident. They're back! Trying to explain their experience.

Isn't it weird? Looks too obscure to me. Wasting away, and that was their policy.

I'm ready to leave, I push the facts in front of me. Facts lost, facts are never what they seem to be. Nothing there! No information left of any kind. Lifting my head, looking for danger signs.

There was a line, there was a formula. Sharp as a knife, facts cut a hole in us.

> I'm still waiting . . .
> I'm still waiting . . .
> I'm still waiting . . .
> I'm still waiting . . .

The feeling returns, whenever we close our eyes. Lifting my head, looking around inside.

The Island of Doubt, it's like the taste of medicine. Working by hindsight, got the message from the oxygen. Making a list, find the cost of opportunity. Doing it right, facts are useless in emergencies.

The feeling returns whenever we close our eyes. Lifting my head, looking around inside.

Facts are simple and facts are straight. Facts are lazy and facts are late. Facts all come with points of view. Facts don't do what I want them to. Facts just twist the truth around. Facts are living turned inside out. Facts are getting the best of them. Facts are nothing on the face of things. Facts don't stain the furniture. Facts go out and slam the door. Facts are written all over your face. Facts continue to change their shape.

> I'm still waiting . . .
> I'm still waiting . . .
> I'm still waiting . . .
> I'm still waiting . . .
> I'm still waiting . . .
> I'm still waiting . . .
> I'm still waiting . . .

AND
SHE WAS

And she was lying in the grass. And she could hear the highway breathing. And she could see a nearby factory. She's making sure she is not dreaming. See the lights of a neighbor's house. Now she's starting to rise. Take a minute to concentrate. She opens up her eyes.

The world was moving, she was right there with it, and she was. The world was moving she was floating above it and she was.

And she was drifting through the backyard. And she was taking off her dress. And she was moving very slowly. Rising up above the earth. Moving into the universe, drifting this way and that. Not touching the ground at all, up above the yard.

The world was moving she was right there with it and she was. The world was moving she was floating above it and she was.

She was glad about it. No doubt about. She isn't sure about where she's gone. No time to think about what to tell them. No time to think about what she's done. (And she was.)

And she was looking at herself. And things were looking like a movie. She had a pleasant elevation. She's moving out in all directions.

The world was moving she was right there with it and she was. The world was moving she was floating above it and she was. Joining the world of missing persons and she was. Missing enough to feel all right and she was.

ONCE IN A LIFETIME

And you may find yourself living in a shotgun shack. And you may find yourself in another part of the world. And you may find yourself behind the wheel of a large automobile. And you may find yourself in a beautiful house, with a beautiful wife. And you may ask yourself, "Well . . . , how did I get here?"

Letting the days go by, let the water hold me down. Letting the day go by, water flowing underground. Into the blue again, after the money's gone. Once in a lifetime, water flowing underground.

And you may ask yourself, "How do I work this?" And you may ask yourself, "Where is that large automobile?" And you may tell yourself, "This is not my beautiful house!" And you may tell yourself, "This is not my beautiful wife!"

Letting the days go by, let the water hold me down. Letting the days go by, water flowing underground. Into the blue again, after the money's gone. Once in a lifetime, water flowing underground.

Same as it ever was . . .

Same as it ever was . . .

Same as it ever was . . .

Same as it ever was . . .

Water dissolving and water removing. There is water at the bottom of the ocean. Carry the water at the bottom of the ocean. Remove the water at the bottom of the ocean!

Letting the days go by, let the water hold me down. Letting the days go by, water flowing underground. Into the blue again, into the silent water. Under the rocks and stone, there is water underground.

Letting the days go by, let the water hold me down. Letting the days go by, water flowing underground. Into the blue again, after the money's gone. Once in a lifetime, water flowing underground.

And you may ask yourself, "What is that beautiful house?" And you may ask yourself, "Where does that highway go to?" And you may ask yourself, "Am I right? . . . Am I wrong?" And you may say to yourself, "MY GOD! . . . WHAT HAVE I DONE?"

Letting the days go by, let the water hold me down. Letting the days go by, water flowing underground. Into the blue again, into the silent water. Under the rocks and stone, there is water underground.

Letting the days go by, let the water hold me down. Letting the days go by, water flowing underground. Into the blue again, after the money's gone. Once in a lifetime, water flowing underground.

Same as it ever was . . .

Same as it ever was . . .

Same as it ever was . . .

Same as it ever was . . .

MARK MAREK

HOUSES

IN

MOTION

For a long time I felt without style or grace, wearing shoes with no socks in cold weather. I knew my heart was in the right place. I knew I'd be able to do these things.

And as we watch him digging his own grave, it was important to know that was where he's at. He can't afford to stop, that is what he believe. He'll keep on digging for a thousand years.

I'm walking a line. I'm thinking about empty motion. I'm walking a line. Just barely enough to be living. Get out of the way. No time to begin. This isn't the time. So nothing was done. Not talking about. Not many at all. I'm turning around. No trouble at all. You notice there's nothing around you, around you. I'm walking a line. Divide and Dissolve.

Never get to say much, never get to talk. Tell us a little bit, but not too much. Right about then is where she give up. She has closed her eyes, she has give up hope.

I turn myself around, I'm moving backwards and forwards. I'm moving twice as much as I was before. I'll keep on digging to the center of the Earth. I'll be down in there, moving in the room!

I'm walking a line. I'm visiting houses in motion. I'm walking a line. Just barely enough to be living. Get out of the way. No time to begin. This isn't the time. So nothing was done. Not talking about. Not many at all. I'm turning around. No trouble at all! Two different houses surround you. I'm walking a line. Divide and Dissolve.

CREATURES OF LOVE

A woman made a man, a man he made a house. And when they lay together, little creatures all come out.

Well, I've seen sex and I think it's all right. It makes those little creatures come to life. I can laugh or I can turn away. Well, I've seen sex and I think it's OK.

We are creatures, creatures of love. We are creatures, creatures of love. From the sleep of reason, a life is born. We are creatures of love, we are creatures of love.

It's OK to be afraid when the blue spark hits your brain. We can love one another, I've been told that it's OK.

Doctor, doctor, tell me what I am. Am I one of those human beings? Well I can laugh or I can learn to think, so help me now to find out what I feel.

We are creatures, creatures of love. We are creatures, creatures of love. We've been here forever, before you were born. We are creatures of love, we are creatures of love.

A man can drive a car and a woman can be a boss. I'm a monkey and a flower. I'm everything at once.

Well, a woman and a man can be together. If they decide to they'll make little creatures. Watch 'em now!

Little creatures of love, with two arms and two legs. From a moment of passion, now they cover the bed.

We are creatures, creatures of love. We are creatures, creatures of love. From the sleep of reason, a life is born. We are creatures of love, we are creatures of love.

THE BIG COUNTRY

I see the shapes, I remember from maps. I see the shoreline, I see the whitecaps. A baseball diamond, nice weather down there. I see the school and the houses where the kids are. Places to park by the factories and buildings. Restaurants and bars for later in the evening.

Then we come to the farmlands, and the undeveloped areas. And I have learned how these things work together. I see the parkway that passes through them all. And I have learned how to look at these things. (AND I SAY):

I wouldn't live there if you paid me. I couldn't live like that, no siree! I couldn't do the things the way those people do. I couldn't live there if you paid me to.

I guess it's healthy, I guess the air is clean. I guess those people have fun with their neighbors and friends. Look at that kitchen and all of that food. Look at them eat it, guess it tastes real good.

They buy it in the farmlands. They bring it to the store. They put it in the car trunks. Then they bring it back home.

I wouldn't live there if you paid me. I couldn't live like that, no siree! I couldn't do the things the way those people do. I wouldn't live there if you paid me to.

I'm tired of looking out the window of the airplane. I'm tired of traveling, I want to be somewhere. It's not even worth talking, about those people down there.

GOO GOO GA GA GA, GOO GOO GA GA GA.

JESSIE HARTLAND

DON'T WORRY ABOUT THE GOVERN– MENT

I see the clouds that move across the sky. I see the wind that moves the clouds away. It moves the clouds over by the building. I pick the building that I want to live in. I smell the pine trees and the peaches in the woods. I see the pinecones that fall by the highway. That's the highway that goes to the building. That's the building that I'm going to live in.

My building has every convenience. It's going to make life easy for me. It's going to be easy to get things done. I will relax, along with my loved ones. Loved ones, visit the building. Take the highway, park, and come up and see me. I'll be working but if you come visit, I'll put down what I'm doing. My friends are important. Don't you worry about me . . . don't you worry about me.

I see the states across this big nation. I see the laws made in Washington, D.C. I think of the ones I consider my favorites. I think of the people that are working for me. Some civil servants are just like my loved ones. They work so hard, and they try to be strong. I'm a lucky guy to live in my building. They all need buildings to help them along.

34

IN THE FUTURE

In the future everyone will have the same haircut and the same clothes.

In the future everyone will be very fat from the starchy diet.

In the future everyone will be very thin from not having enough to eat.

In the future it will be next to impossible to tell girls from boys, even in bed.

In the future men will be "super-masculine" and women will be "ultra-feminine."

In the future atomic fusion will enable us to build a skyscraper with the energy obtained from a grain of salt.

In the future through genetic surgery there will be a race of menial workers, studs, "whores," TV personalities and politicians.

In the future half of us will be "mentally ill."

In the future there will be no religion or spiritualism of any sort.

In the future the "psychic arts" will be put to practical use.

In the future we will not think that "nature" is beautiful.

In the future the weather will always be the same (relative to the way it is now).

In the future no one will fight with anyone else because anyone can be anything he or she wants to be.

In the future there will be an atomic war that will reduce the survivors to savages.

In the future water will be expensive.

In the future all material items will be free.

In the future everyone's house will be like a little fortress.

In the future everyone will think about love all the time.

In the future TV will be so good that the printed word will function as an artform only.

In the future people with boring jobs will take pills to relieve boredom.

In the future everyone but the wealthy will be very happy.

In the future everyone but the wealthy will be very filthy.

In the future everyone but the wealthy will be very healthy.

In the future communication/distribution systems will be so good that no one will live in cities.

In the future farming will be managed through a nationwide computer hookup.

In the future there will be mini-wars going on everywhere.

In the future political and other decisions will be based completely on opinion polls.

In the future only the very wealthy will be able to travel or move out of their houses.

In the future individuals with aggressive inclinations will go out for "killer" sports.

In the future there will be machines which will produce a religious experience in the user.

In the future there will be a classless society, no one richer than anyone else.

In the future people will constantly be having plastic surgery, altering their features many times during a lifetime.

In the future there will be many mass suicides.

In the future there will be groups of wild people, living in the wilderness, who will rob suburbanites.

In the future there will be only paper money which will be personalized.

In the future everyone will only get to go home once a year.

In the future everyone will stay home all the time.

In the future we will not have time for leisure activities.

In the future we will only "work" one day a week.

In the future our bodies will be shriveled up (but healthy) and our brains will be bigger.

In the future there will be starving people everywhere.

In the future no one will be able to afford TV or newspapers, resulting in no one knowing what's going on.

In the future people will live in space.

In the future only the very wealthy will have pets.

In the future the poor will be regulated by the rich.

In the future the crippled, retarded, and helpless will be killed.

In the future everyone's house will be a total entertainment center, with video, pills, dancing, sex tools, holographic movies, and game machines.

In the future everyone will have his or her own individual style of very way-out clothes.

In the future we will all eat our favorite foods, only they will all be synthetic.

In the future we will fuck anything, anytime, anywhere.

In the future there will be so much going on that no one will be able to keep track of it.

KRZYSZTOF WODICZKO

CITIES

Think of London, a small city. It's dark, dark in the daytime. The people sleep, sleep in the daytime. If they want to, if they want to.

I'm checking them out, I'm checking them out. I got it figured out, I got it figured out. There's good points, some bad points. It all works out, you know I'm a little freaked out. Find a city, find myself a city to live in. Find a city, find myself a city to live in.

There are a lot of rich people in Birmingham. A lot of ghosts in a lot of houses. Look over there! A dry ice factory. A good place to get some thinking done.

I'm checking it out, I'm checking it out. I got it figured out, I got it figured out. There's good points, some bad points. It all works out, you know I'm a little *freaked* out. Find a city, find myself a city to live in. Find a city, find myself a city to live in.

Down El Paso way things get pretty spread out. People got no idea where in the world they are. They go up north and come back south. Still got no idea where in the world they are.

Did I forget to mention, forget to mention Memphis? Home of Elvis and the ancient Greeks. Do I smell? I smell home cooking. It's only the river, it's only the river.

I'm checking them out, I'm checking them out. I got it figured out, I got it figured out. There's good points, some bad points. It all works out, you know I'm a little freaked out. Find a city, find myself a city to live in. Find a city, find myself a city to live in.

MY BIG HANDS (Fall Through the Cracks)

Well, it ain't *my* fault, my fault that things gone wrong. And it ain't my fault, some things are sticking out. My big hands. Keep my big hands to myself. Tiptoe too, tiptoe around the house.

Come, come on in. It's not, it's not like that. Down, down we go. Fall through, fall through the cracks.

Well, I help myself, help myself to what I want. Side by side, get stupid in the dark. Didn't get home, things broke down. No sense, not at all.

Come, come on in. It's not, it's not like that. Down, down we go. Fall through, fall through the cracks.

A MAN CAN'T KNOW WHAT IT'S LIKE TO BE A MOTHER
A STRONG SENSE OF DUTY IMPRISONS YOU
ABSOLUTE SUBMISSION CAN BE A FORM OF FREEDOM
ABUSE OF POWER COMES AS NO SURPRISE
ACTION CAUSES MORE TROUBLE THAN THOUGHT
ALIENATION PRODUCES ECCENTRICS OR REVOLUTIONARIES
ALL THINGS ARE DELICATELY INTERCONNECTED
AN ELITE IS INEVITABLE
ANY SURPLUS IS IMMORAL
AT TIMES INACTIVITY IS PREFERABLE TO MINDLESS FUNCTIONING
BOREDOM MAKES YOU DO CRAZY THINGS
CATEGORIZING FEAR IS CALMING
CHILDREN ARE THE CRUELEST OF ALL
CHILDREN ARE THE HOPE OF THE FUTURE
CLASS ACTION IS A NICE IDEA WITH NO SUBSTANCE
CLASS STRUCTURE IS AS ARTIFICIAL AS PLASTIC
CRIME AGAINST PROPERTY IS RELATIVELY UNIMPORTANT
DECADENCE CAN BE AN END IN ITSELF
DEVIANTS ARE SACRIFICED TO INCREASE GROUP SOLIDARITY
DREAMING WHILE AWAKE IS A FRIGHTENING CONTRADICTION
EATING TOO MUCH IS CRIMINAL
EVEN YOUR FAMILY CAN BETRAY YOU
EXPIRING FOR LOVE IS BEAUTIFUL BUT STUPID
FAKE OR REAL INDIFFERENCE IS A POWERFUL PERSONAL WEAPON
FATHERS OFTEN USE TOO MUCH FORCE
FREEDOM IS A LUXURY NOT A NECESSITY
HIDING YOUR MOTIVES IS DESPICABLE
HUMANISM IS OBSOLETE
HUMOR IS A RELEASE
IF YOU AREN'T POLITICAL YOUR PERSONAL LIFE SHOULD BE EXEMPLARY
IT'S BETTER TO BE NAIVE THAN JADED
IT'S IMPORTANT TO STAY CLEAN ON ALL LEVELS
IT'S NOT GOOD TO LIVE ON CREDIT
KILLING IS UNAVOIDABLE BUT IS NOTHING TO BE PROUD OF
LACK OF CHARISMA CAN BE FATAL
LOVING ANIMALS IS A SUBSTITUTE ACTIVITY
MONEY CREATES TASTE
MURDER HAS ITS SEXUAL SIDE
OPACITY IS AN IRRESISTIBLE CHALLENGE
PRIVATE PROPERTY CREATED CRIME
PUSH YOURSELF TO THE LIMIT AS OFTEN AS POSSIBLE
RAISE BOYS AND GIRLS THE SAME WAY
RANDOM MATING IS GOOD FOR DEBUNKING SEX MYTHS
REVOLUTION BEGINS WITH CHANGES IN THE INDIVIDUAL
STARVATION IS NATURE'S WAY
STUPID PEOPLE SHOULDN'T BREED
THE MOST PROFOUND THINGS ARE INEXPRESSIBLE
THE WORLD OPERATES ACCORDING TO DISCOVERABLE LAWS
WAR IS A PURIFICATION RITE
YOU ARE A VICTIM OF THE RULES YOU LIVE BY
YOU ARE GUILELESS IN YOUR DREAMS
YOUR OLDEST FEARS ARE THE WORST ONES

TENTATIVE DECISIONS

Now that I can release my tension, let me make clear my best intention.

Girls ask: can I define decision?

Boys ask: can I describe their function?

The boys want to talk, would like to talk about those problems.

The girls say they are concerned, (that they are) concerned with decisiveness.

It's a hard logic to follow, and the girls get lost. And the boys say they're concerned, (that they are) concerned with decisiveness.

(I want to talk) I'm going to talk as much as I want. (I'm going to give) I'm going to give the problem to you.

Decide, decide, make up your mind. Decide, decide, I told you what to say.

Confuse, confuse, describe what I found. Confuse, confuse, I told you what to say.

The girls want to talk, would like to talk about those problems.

The boys say they are concerned, (that they are) concerned with decisiveness.

It's a hard logic to follow, and the boys get lost. And the girls say they're concerned (that they are) concerned with decisiveness.

(I want to talk) I'm going to talk as much as I want. (I'm going to give) I'm going to give the problem to you.

Decide, decide, make up your mind. Decide, decide, I told you what to say.

Confuse, confuse, describe what I found. Confuse, confuse, I told you what to say.

We get exploded because they've got

money and God in their pockets

BARBARA KRUGER

WARNING SIGN

Warning sign, warning sign (I see it but I pay it no mind). Hear my voice, hear my voice (it's saying something and it's not very nice). Pay attention, pay attention (I'm talking to you and I hope you're concentrating). I've got money now, I've got money now (Come on, baby, come on, baby.)

Warning sign of things to come (take it over, take it over). Someone's talking on my telephone (when we're older, when we're older). Hear my voice, move my hair. (I move it around a lot, but I don't care what I remember.)

Warning sign, warning sign (look at my hair, I like the design). It's the truth, it's the truth (your glassy eyes and your open mouth). Take it easy, take it easy (it's a natural thing and you have to relax). I've got money now, I've got money now (Come on, baby, come on, baby).

Warning sign of things to come (turn me over, turn me over). Love is here but I guess it's gone now (hurry up, babe, hurry up, babe). Hear my voice, move my hair. (I move it around a lot, but I don't care.)

Do you remember? What is it that you remember? Baby remember, baby remember.

SUE COE

LISTENING WIND

Mojique sees his village from a nearby hill. Mojique thinks of days before Americans came. He sees the foreigners in growing numbers. He sees the foreigners in fancy houses. He thinks of days that he can still remember now.

Mojique holds a package in his quivering hands. Mojique sends the package to the American man. Softly, he glides along the streets and alleys. Up comes the wind that makes them run for cover. He feels the time is surely now or never more.

The wind in my heart, the wind in my heart. The dust in my head, the dust in my head. The wind in my heart, the wind in my heart. Come to drive them away, drive them away.

Mojique buys equipment in the marketplace. Mojique plants devices in the free trade zone. He feels the wind is lifting up his people. He calls the wind to guide him on his mission. He knows his friend the wind is always standing by.

Mojique smells the wind that comes from far away. Mojique waits for news in a quiet place. He feels the presence of the wind around him. He feels the power of the past behind him. He has the knowledge of the wind to guide him on.

The wind in my heart, the wind in my heart. The dust in my head, the dust in my head. The wind in my heart, the wind in my heart. Come to drive them away, drive them away.

SOCIAL STUDIES

I thought that if I ate the food of the area I was visiting that I might assimilate the point of view of the people there, as if the point of view was somehow in the food.

So I would make no choices myself regarding what I ate. I would simply follow the examples of those around me. I would study menus very carefully, making note of important differences and similarities.

When shopping at the supermarket, I felt a great desire to walk off with someone else's groceries so I could study them at length and study their effects on me. As though if I ate their groceries I would become that person, until I finished their groceries.

And we might find ourselves going to the same places. Running into one another at the movies, or in a shopping mall. Reading the same books. Watching the same TV programs. Wearing the same clothes. Traveling to the same places, and taking the same pictures. Getting sick at the same time, and getting well again simultaneously. Finding ourselves attracted to the same people. Working at the same job, and making the same amount of money. Living identical lives as long as the groceries lasted.

LYNDA BARRY

GIVE ME BACK MY NAME

There's a word for it, and words don't mean a thing. There's a name for it, and names make all the difference in the world.

Some things can never be spoken. Some things cannot be pronounced. That word does not exist in any language. It will never be uttered by a human mouth.

Let X make a statement. Let breath pass through those cracked lips. That man was my hero, and now that word has been taken from us.

Some things can never be spoken. Some things cannot be pronounced. That word does not exist in any language. It will never be uttered by a human mouth.

Give me back my name. Give me back my name. Something has been changed in my life. Something has been changed in my life. Something must be returned to us. Something must be returned to us.

Mr. CAZZIE RUSSELL
Inches 370 pounds capable

February

Mr GEORGE Gittens
feet 179 pounds CAPABLE
pounds 256 (Strength) 736)

Mr. FLOyd PATTERSON
inches 295 pounds capable

West 36th St

Mr. RONALd (SAYERS)
inches 127 pounds capable

north Teaneck, N.J.

51

SEEN AND NOT SEEN

He would see faces; in movies, on TV, in magazines and in books: he thought that some of these faces might be right for him. And through the years, by keeping an ideal facial structure fixed in his mind, or somewhere in the back of his mind, that he might, by force of will, cause his face to approach those of his ideal. The change would be very subtle. It might take ten years or so. Gradually, his face would change its shape: a more hooked nose, wider, thinner lips, beady eyes, a larger forehead.

He imagined that this was an ability he shared with most other people. They had also molded their faces according to some ideal. Maybe they imagined that their new face would better suit their personality. Or maybe they imagined that their personality would be forced to change to fit the new appearance. *This* is why first impressions are often correct.

Some people might have made mistakes. They may have arrived at an appearance that bears no relationship to them. They may have picked an ideal appearance based on some childish whim or momentary impulse. Some may have gotten halfway there, and then changed their minds.

He wonders if he, too, might have made a similar mistake.

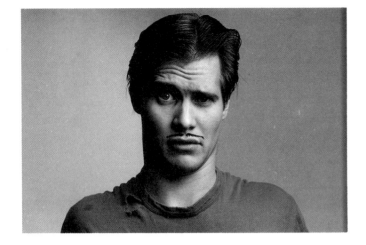

2

3

4

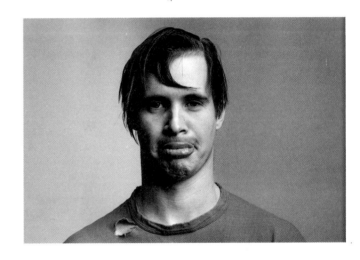

5

6

Duane Michals

LIFE DURING WARTIME

Heard of a van that is loaded with weapons, packed up and ready to go. Heard of some gravesites out by the highway, a place where nobody knows. The sound of gunfire, off in the distance, I'm getting used to it now. Lived in a brownstone, lived in a ghetto, I've lived all over this town.

This ain't no party, this ain't no disco, this ain't no fooling around. No time for dancing, or lovey dovey. I ain't got time for that now.

Transmit the message to the receiver, hope for an answer some day. I got three passports, a couple of visas. You don't even know my real name. High on a hillside the trucks are loading, everything's ready to roll. I sleep in the daytme, I work in the nighttime, I might not ever get home.

This ain't no party, this ain't no disco, this ain't no fooling around. This ain't the Mudd Club, or C.B.G.B., I ain't got time for that now.

Heard about Houston? Heard about Detroit? Heard about Pittsburgh, P.A.? You oughta know not to stand by the window, somebody see you up there. I got some groceries, some peanut butter, to last a couple of days. I ain't got no speakers, ain't got no headphones, ain't got no records to play.

Why stay in college? Why go to night school? Gonna be different this time. Can't write a letter, can't send a postcard, I can't write nothing at all.

This ain't no party, this ain't no disco, this ain't no fooling around. I'd like to kiss you, I'd love to hold you, I ain't got time for that now.

Trouble in transit, got through the roadblock, we blended in with the crowd. We got computers, we're tapping phone lines, I know that that ain't allowed. We dress like students, we dress like housewives, or in a suit and a tie. I changed my hairstyle so many times now, I don't know what I look like! You make me shiver, I feel so tender, we make a pretty good team. Don't get exhausted, I'll do some driving, you ought to get some sleep. Get your instructions, follow directions, then you should change your address. Maybe tomorrow, maybe the next day, whatever you think is best. Burned all my notebooks, what good are notebooks? They won't help me survive. My chest is aching, burns like a furnace, the burning keeps me alive. Try to stay healthy, physical fitness, don't want to catch no disease. Try to be careful, don't take no chances, you better watch what you say. . . .

I'M NOT IN LOVE

. . . Pretty! What is? Brand new? Well that's not the way I think of you. You'll touch me, in a minute; but that's not what I want to do.

We are two strangers, we might never have met. We can talk forever, I understand what you said.

But I'm not in love. What does it take to really fall in love? Do people really fall in love?

. . . Happy? Is there time for this? Is this responsibility? Girl time, boy time. Is that the difference between me and you?

I won't ask any questions, who needs a new start? I choose to believe you, I said before that I can't . . .

. . . 'Cause I'm not in love. What does it take to fall in love? Why would I want to fall in love?

JACK BUTLER

LOVE →
BUILDING
ON FIRE

When my love stands next to your love, I can't define love when it's not love. It's not love, it's not love. Which is my face, which is a building, which is on fire.

When my love stands next to your love, I can't define love when it's not love. It's not love, it's not love. Which is my face, which is a building, which is on fire.

I've got two loves. I've got two loves. And they go tweet, tweet, tweet, tweet, tweet, tweet like little birds.

They're my two loves . . . count them one, two loves . . . count them one, two loves. Which is my face, which is a building, which is on fire.

It's not love. It's not love. Which is my face, which is a building, which is on fire.

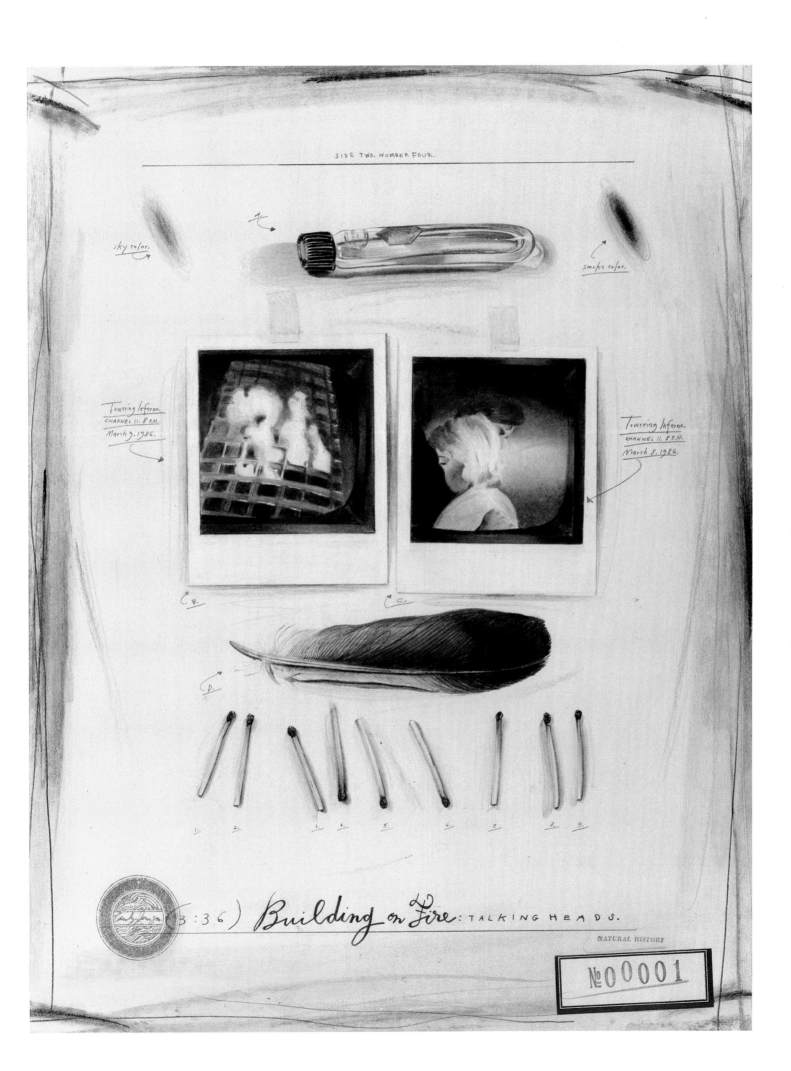

SLIPPERY PEOPLE

What about the time you were rolling over? Fall on your face, you must be having fun.

Walk lightly! Think of a time. You'd best believe this thing is real.

Put away that gun, this part is simple. Try to recognize what is in your mind.

God help us! Help us lose our minds. These slippery people, help us understand.

What's the matter with him?

He's all right! I see his face . . . the Lord won't mind. Don't play no games . . . he's all right. Love from the bottom to the top. Turn like a wheel . . . he's all right. See for yourself . . . the Lord won't mind. We're gonna move . . . right now. Turn like a wheel inside a wheel.

I remember when, sitting in the tub. Pulled out the plug, the water was running out.

Cool down, stop acting crazy.

They're gonna leave and we'll be on our own.

Seven times five, they were living creatures. Watch them come to life, right before your eyes.

Backsliding! How do you do? These slippery people gonna see you through.

What's the matter with him . . . ? He's all right! How do you know . . . ? The Lord won't mind. Don't know no games . . . he's all right. Love from the bot-

tom to the top. Turn like a wheel
inside a wheel.

What's the matter with him
. . . ? He's all right! I see his face
. . . the Lord won't mind. Don't
play no games . . . he's all right!
And we're going to the top.

Turn like a wheel . . . he's all
right. See for yourself . . . the
Lord won't mind. We're gonna
move . . . right now. Turn like a
wheel inside a wheel.

BORN UNDER PUNCHES (The Heat Goes On)

Take a look at these hands. Take a look at these hands. The hand speaks. The hand of a Government Man. Well, I'm a tumbler. Born under punches. I'm so thin.

All I want is to breathe. (I'm too thin.) Won't you breathe with me? Find a little space, so we move in between and keep one step ahead of yourself.

Don't you miss it, don't you miss it. Some a you people just about missed it! Last time to make plans! Well, I'm a tumbler, I'm a Government Man.

Never seen anything like that before. Falling bodies tumble across the floor. (Well, I'm a tumbler!) When you get to where you want to be. (Thank you! Thank you!) When you get to where you want to be. (Don't even mention it!)

Take a look at these hands. They're passing in between us. Take a look at these hands. Take a look at these hands. You don't have to mention it. No thanks. I'm a Government Man.

And the heat goes on . . .
And the heat goes on . . .
And the heat goes on . . .
And the heat goes on . . .

I'm not a drowning man! And I'm not a burning building! (I'm a tumbler!) Drowning cannot hurt a man! Fire cannot hurt a man. (Not the Government Man.)

All I want to do is breathe. Thank you. (Thank you.) Won't you breathe with me? Find a little space so we move in between. (I'm so thin.) And keep one step ahead of yourself. (I'm catching up with myself.)

All I want is to breathe. Won't you breathe with me? (Hands of a Government Man.) Find a little space so we move in between. And keep one step ahead of yourself. (Don't you miss it! Don't you miss it!)

And the heat goes on . . .
And the heat goes on . . .
And the heat goes on . . .
And the heat goes on . . .

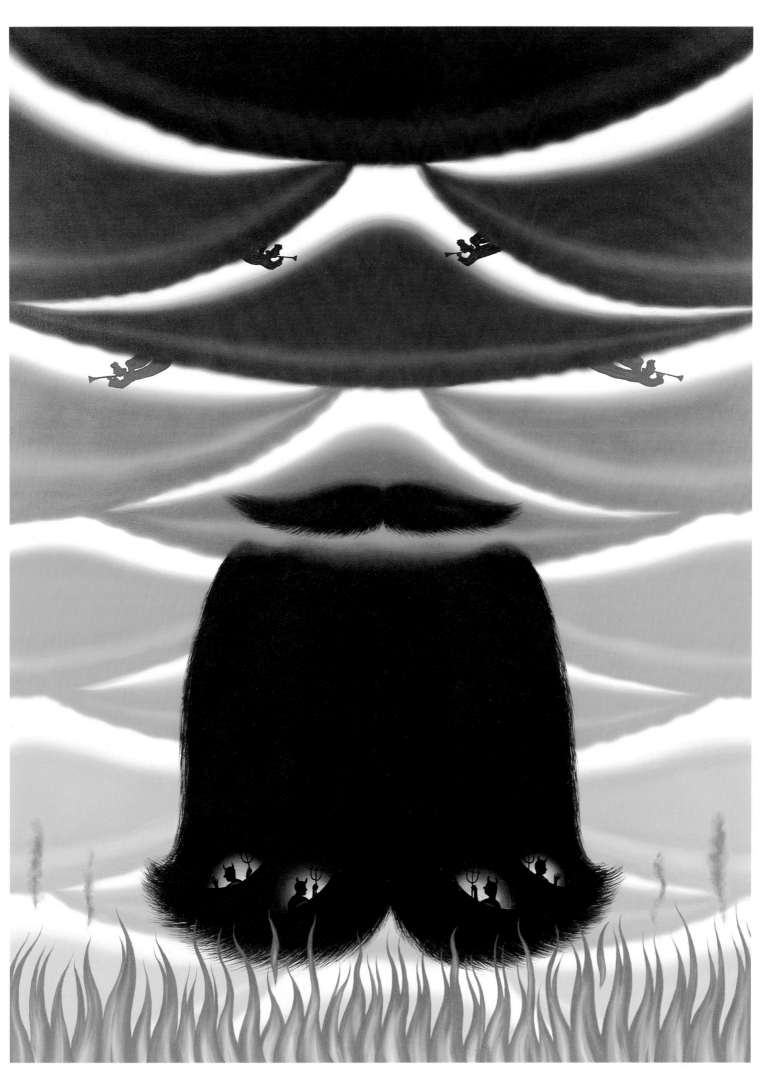

GIRLFRIEND IS BETTER

Who took the money? Who took the money away? It's always showtime here at the edge of the stage. I wake up and wonder, what was the place, what was the time? We want to wait, but here we go again . . .

Takes over slowly, but doesn't last very long. No need to worry, everything's under control. O-U-T but no hard feelings. What do you know? Take you away. We're being taken for a ride again.

I got a girlfriend that's better than that, she's got the smoke in her eyes. She's moving up, going right through my heart. She's gonna give me surprise. Better than this, know that it's right. I think you can if you like. I got a girlfriend with bows in her hair, and nothing is better than that.

Down in the basement we hear the sound of machines. I'm driving in circles, come to my senses sometimes. Why start it over? Nothing was lost, everything's free. I don't care how impossible it seems.

Somebody calls you but you cannot hear, get closer to be far away. Only one look, and that's all that we need. Maybe that's all that it takes. All that it takes, all that it takes. All that it takes, all that it takes. I got a girlfriend that's better than *that*, and she goes wherever she likes.

I got a girlfriend that's better than that, now everyone's getting involved. She's moving up, going right through my heart. We might not ever get caught. Going right through (try to stay cool). Going through, staying cool. I got a girlfriend that's better than that, and nothing is better than you.

I got a girlfriend that's better than this, and you don't remember at all. As we get older and stop making sense, you won't find her waiting long. Stop Making Sense, Stop Making Sense. . . . Stop making sense, making sense. I got a girlfriend that's better than that, and nothing is better than this.

TELEVISION MAN

I'm looking and I'm dreaming for the first time. I'm inside and I'm outside at the same time. And everything is real. Do I like the way I feel?

The world crashes in, into my living room. Television made me what I am. People like to put the television down, but we are just good friends. I'm a television man.

I knew a girl, she was a macho man. But it's all right, I wasn't fooled for long. This is the place for me. I'm the king and you're the queen.

The world crashes in, into my living room. Television made me what I am. People like to put the television down, but we are just good friends. I'm a television man.

Take a walk in the beautiful garden. Everyone would like to say hello. It doesn't matter what you say. Come and take us away.

The world crashes in, into my living room. The world crashes in, into my living room. The world crashes in, into my living room. The world crashes in, into my living room.

And we are still good friends . . . (television man). I'm watching everything . . . (television man). Television man . . . (I'm watching everything) . . . television man. We are still good friends. I'm trying to be watching everything, I got to say we are still good friends. You know the way it is. (Television man.) I've got what you need. We are still good friends. I know the way you are television man. I know you're trying to be watching everything, and I got to say, that's how the story ends.

NAM JUNE PAIK

FOUND A JOB

"Damn that television . . . what a bad picture!"

"Don't get upset, it's not a major disaster."

"There's nothing on tonight," he said, "I don't know what's the matter."

"Nothing's ever on," she said, "so I don't know why you bother."

We've heard this little scene, we've heard it many times. People fighting over little things and wasting precious time. They might be better off—I think—the way it seems to me, making up their own shows, which might be better than TV.

Judy's in the bedroom, inventing situations. Bob is on the street today, scouting up locations. They've enlisted all their family. They've enlisted all their friends. It helped save their relationship, and made it work again. . . .

Their show gets real high ratings. They think they have a hit. There might even be a spinoff, but they're not sure about that. If they ever watch TV again it'd be too soon for them. Bob never yells about the picture now, he's having too much fun.

Judy's in the bedroom, inventing situations. Bob is on the street today, scouting up locations. They've enlisted all their family. They've enlisted all their friends. It helped save their relationship, and made it work again. . . .

So think about this little scene, apply it to your life. If your work isn't what you love, then something isn't right. Just look at Bob and Judy. They're happy as can be. Inventing situations, putting them on TV.

Judy's in the bedroom, inventing situations. Bob is on the street today, scouting up locations. They've enlisted all their family. They've enlisted all their friends. It helped save their relationship, and made it work again. . . .

PAPER

Hold the paper up to the light (some rays pass right through). Expose yourself out there for a minute (some rays pass right through).

Take a little rest when the rays pass through. Take a little time off when the rays pass through. Go ahead and mix it up . . . go ahead and tie it up, in a long distance telephone call.

Hold on to that paper. Hold on to that paper. Hold on because it's been taken care of. Hold on to that paper.

See if you can fit it on the paper. See if you can get it on the paper. See if you can fit it on the paper. See if you can get it on the paper.

Had a love affair but it was only paper (some rays they passed right through). Had a lot of fun, could have been a lot better (some rays they passed right through).

Take a little consideration, take every combination. Take a few weeks off, make it tighter, tighter. But it was never, it was never written down. Still might be a chance that it might work out.

Hold on to that paper. Hold on to that paper. Hold on, because it'll be taken care of. Hold on to that paper.

Don't think I can fit it on the paper. Don't think I can get it on the paper. Go ahead and rip up the paper. Go ahead and tear up the paper.

STUDIO DUMBAR

AIR

Air hit me in the face. I run faster, faster into the air. I say to myself, "Where is that protection that I needed?"

Air can hurt you too. Air can hurt you too. Some people say not to worry about the air. Some people never had experience with air.

Air, it can break your heart. So remember, when the weather gets rough you'll say to yourself, "What is happening to my skin? Where is that protection that I needed?"

Air can hurt you too. Air can hurt you too. Some people say not to worry about the air. Some people don't know shit about the air.

MOON ROCKS

Flying saucers. Levitation. Yo! *I* could do that! Get ready, for heavy duty. Go on, give it a chance. Give it a chance, give it a chance. I saw your hair start to curl. So get up, write it down. You better wait for a while.

So take your hands out of your pockets and get your face adjusted. I heard it, somebody lied. And I'm staring out the window. Going to let this thing continue, in its natural time. Roundheads, Squareheads. Get settled in. You can hear my belly rumble, there's a voice that starts to mumble. Woo! It's starting to sing.

Protons, neutrons. I ate a rock from the moon. Got shocked once, shocked twice. Let's see what it can do. Man in the moon, moon in the man. I got a rock in my throat. Upside, upside down. My tummy starts to talk . . . (what it say?)

"Gonna rock it till I shock it. Gonna kick it till I drop it. Woo! Love at first sight. You can kick it, you can poke it. I think I broke it. What about that? Skin from a snake, blood from a stone. You know that ain't no lie. I got hundreds of expressions, try to make a good impression. Woo! Right between the eyes."

I don't mind, let me go. Sounds inside, I don't know. Let me be, why not stay? I feel numb, let me play.

I got wild imagination, talkin' transubstantiation. (Any version will do.) I got mass communication, I'm the human corporation. I ate a rock from the moon. Moon in the rock, rock in the moon. There's a moon in my throat. You might think I'm wasting time, you might laugh, but not for long. Hey! I'm working it out!

FRANK OLINSKY

ARTISTS ONLY

WORDS BY WAYNE ZIEVE

I'm painting. I'm painting again. I'm painting, I'm painting again. I'm cleaning, I'm cleaning my brain.

Pretty soon now, I will be bitter. Pretty soon now, will be a quitter. Pretty soon now, I will be bitter. You can't see it till it's finished.

I don't have to prove . . . that I am creative! I don't have to prove . . . that I am creative! All my pictures are confused. And now I'm going to take me to you.

DRUGS

And all I see is little dots. Some are smeared and some are spots. Feels like murder but that's all right. Somebody said there's too much light. Pull down the shade and it's all right. It'll be over in a minute or two.

I'm charged up . . . don't put me down. Don't feel like talking . . . don't mess around. I feel mean . . . I feel OK. I'm charged up . . . electricity.

The boys are making a big mess. This makes the girls all start to laugh. (I don't know what they're talking about.) The boys are worried, the girls are shocked. They pick the sound and let it drop. Nobody knows what they're talking about!

I'm charged up . . . I'm kinda wooden. I'm barely moving . . . I study motion. I study myself . . . I fooled myself! I'm charged up . . . it's pretty intense.

I'm charged up . . . don't put me down. Don't feel like talking . . . don't mess around. I feel mean . . . I feel OK. I'm charged up . . . electricity.

GARY PANTER

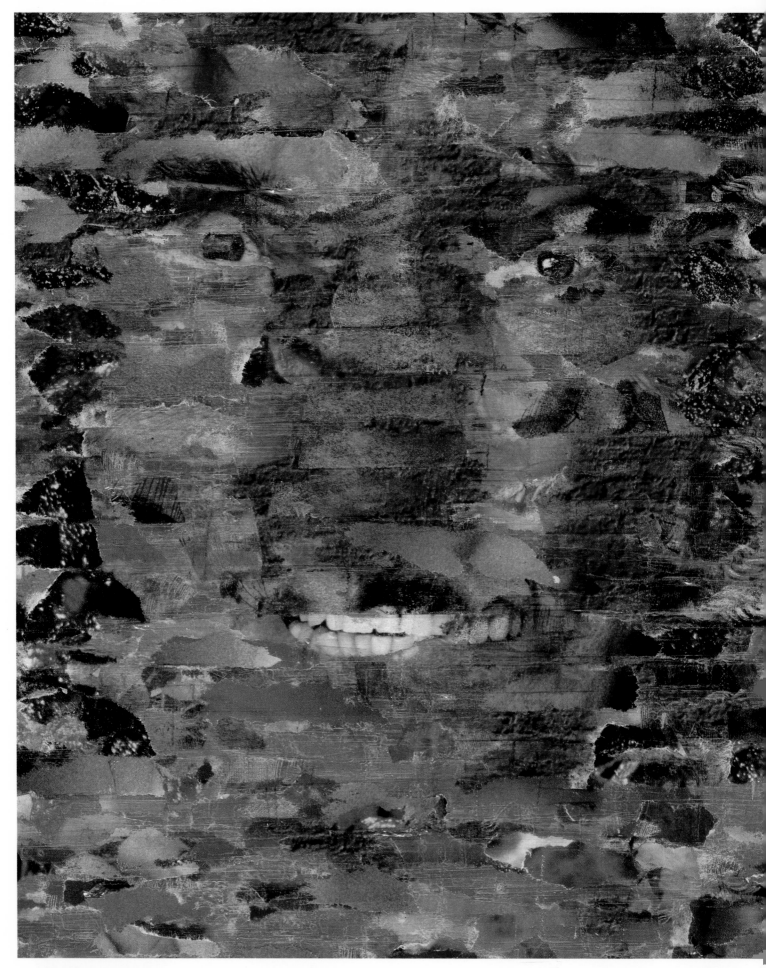

PSYCHO KILLER

I can't seem to face up to the facts. I'm tense and nervous and I can't relax. I can't sleep because my bed's on fire. Don't touch me I'm a real live wire.

Psycho killer, qu'est-ce que c'est?

Fa fa fa fa fa fa. Better run away. Psycho killer, qu'est-ce que c'est?

Fa fa fa fa fa fa. Better run away . . .

I passed out hours ago. I'm sadder than you'll ever know. I close my eyes on this sunny day. Say something once, why say it again?

You start a conversation, you can't even finish it! You're talking

WORDS BY DAVID BYRNE, CHRIS FRANTZ AND TINA WEYMOUTH

a lot, but you're not saying anything! When *I* have nothing to say, my lips are sealed. Say something once, why say it again?

Psycho killer, qu'est-ce que c'est?

Fa fa fa fa fa fa. Better run away. Psycho killer, qu'est-ce que c'est?

Fa fa fa fa fa fa. Better run away.

Ce que j'ai fais, ce soir la. Ce

quelle a dit, ce soir la. Realisant mon espoir, je me lance, vers la gloire . . . OK.

We are vain and we are blind. I hate people when they're not polite. Psycho killer, qu'est-ce que

c'est?

Fa fa fa fa fa fa. Better run away. Psycho killer, qu'est-ce que c'est?

Fa fa fa fa fa fa. Better run away.

THE OVERLOAD

A terrible signal, too weak to even recognize. A gentle collapsing, the removal of the insides. I'm touched by your pleas. I value these moments. We're older than we realize . . . In someone's eyes.

A frequent returning and leaving unnoticed. A condition of mercy. A change in the weather.

A view to remember. The center is missing. They question how the future lies . . . In someone's eyes.

The gentle collapsing of every surface. We travel on the quiet road . . . The overload.

RUSSELL MILLS

BURNING DOWN THE HOUSE

Watch out, you might get what you're after. Cool babies, strange but not a stranger. I'm an ordinary guy, burning down the house.

Hold tight, wait till the party's over. Hold tight, we're in for nasty weather. There has got to be a way, burning down the house.

Here's your ticket, pack your bags, time for jumping overboard. . . . The transportation is here. Close enough, but not too far, maybe you know where you are: Fighting fire with fire.

All wet, hey you might need a raincoat. Shakedown, dreams walking in broad daylight. Three hundred sixty-five degrees, burning down the house.

It was once upon a place, sometimes I listen to myself. Gonna come in first place. People on their way to work, baby, what did you expect? Gonna burst into flame.

My house, out of the ordinary. That's right, don't want to hurt nobody. Some things sure can sweep me off my feet. Burning down the house.

No visible means of support, and you have not seen nothing yet. Everything's stuck together. I don't know what you expect, staring into the TV set. Fighting fire with fire.

I ZIMBRA

WORDS BY HUGO BALL

Gadji beri, bimba clandridi, lauli lonni, cadori gadjam. A bim beri, glassala glandride, e glassala, tuffm i zimbra.

Bim blassa, galassasa zimbrabim. Blassa gallassasa zimbrabim.

A bim beri, glassala gladrid, e glassala, tuffm i zimbra.

Gadji beri, bimba glandrid, lauli lonni, cadori gadjam. A bim beri, glassala glandride, e glassala, tuffm i zimbra.

JEAN-MICHEL BASQUIAT

MIND

Time won't change you. Money won't change you. I haven't got the faintest idea. Everything seems to be up in the air at this time.

I need something to change your mind.

Drugs won't change you. Religion won't change you. Science won't change you. Looks like I can't change you.

I try to talk to you, to make things clear. But you're not even listening to me. (And it comes directly from my heart to you).

I need something to change your mind.

THE GOOD THING

I will fight, will fight with my heart. I will fight, will fight with understanding. In my mind, the weather never changes. Skill overcomes difficult situations.

A straight line exists between me and the good thing. I have found the line and its direction is known to me. Absolute trust keeps me going in the right direction. Any intrusion is met with a heart full of the good thing.

Try to compare what I am presenting. You will meet with much frustration. Try to find similar situation. You will always find the same solution.

As the heart finds the good thing, the feeling is multiplied. Add the will to the strength, and it equals conviction. As we economize, efficiency is multiplied. To the extent I am determined . . . the result is the Good Thing.

I have adopted this and made it my own: CUT BACK THE WEAKNESS, REINFORCE WHAT IS STRONG.

WILLIAM T. WILEY

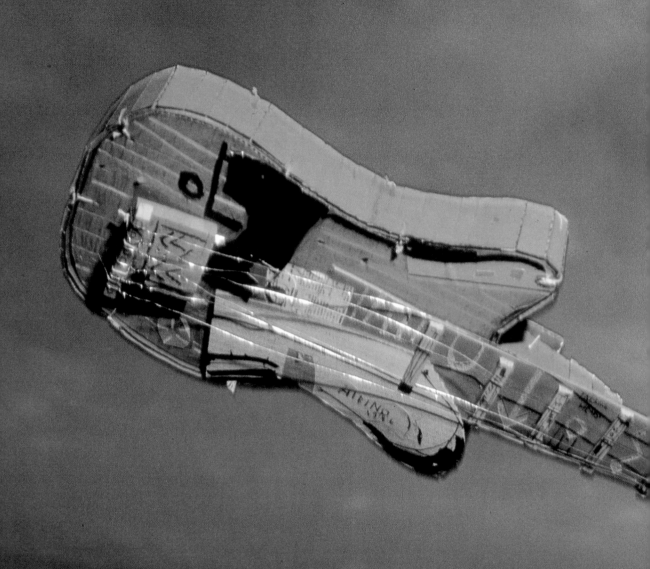

ELECTRIC GUITAR

Electric guitar gets run over by a car on the highway. This is a crime against the state. This is the meaning of life:

To tune this electric guitar.

An electric guitar is brought into a court of law. The judge and jury (twelve members of the jury) all listening to records. This is a crime against the state. This is the verdict they reach:

Never listen to electric guitar.

Electric guitar is copied, the copy sounds better. Call this law and justice, call this freedom and liberty? I perjure myself, right in front of the jury!

Is this a crime against the state? No! This is the verdict they reach:

Someone controls electric guitar.

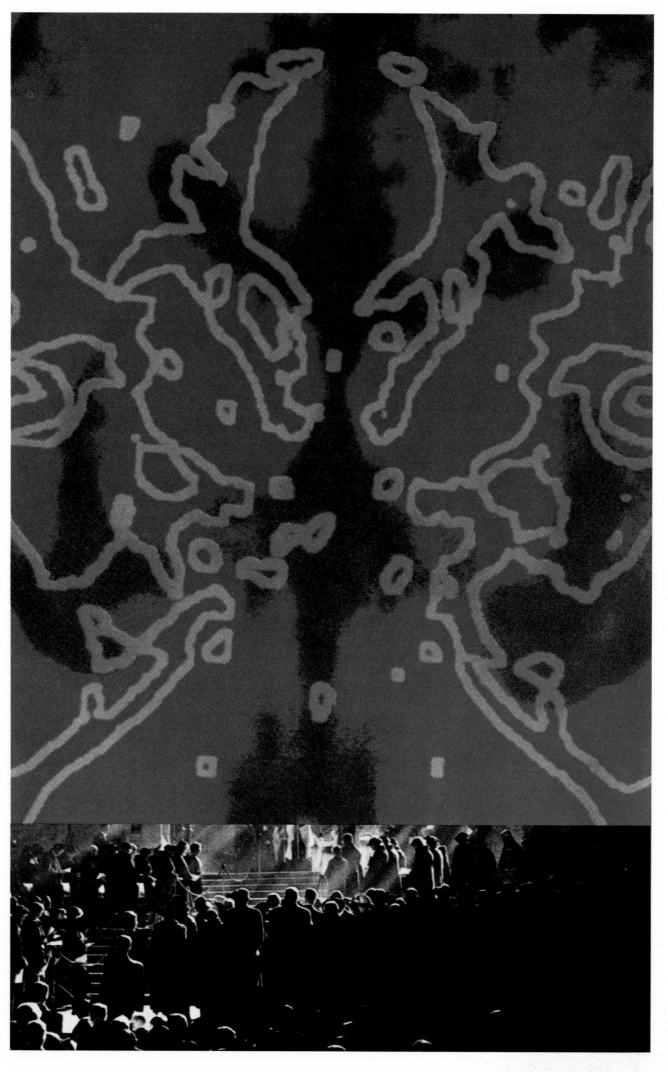

WALK IT DOWN

I am just a number. I hang on to what I got. You say what you want to. I just try to stay alive. I put myself together. People say, get away, somebody will turn you in.

Life without surrender. Togetherness . . . ecstasy is what I need. I can laugh, but I should cry, when love and understanding are the ultimate crimes.

Walk it down. Talk it down. Sympathy. Luxury. Somebody will take you there. Walk it down. Talk it down. Sympathy. Luxury. Somebody will take you there.

She says she remembers. Time, a long time ago. We belong together. I turn up the radio. Lies, and propaganda. I'm gonna tell you what I need.

Life without surrender. Togetherness . . . ecstasy is what I need. I got yours and you got mine. And I can swim, but I should fly.

Walk it down. Talk it down. Sympathy. Luxury. Somebody will take you there. Walk it down. Talk it down. Sympathy. Luxury. Somebody will take you there.

Ain't no crime to believe. I took my money, I bet my life. What you see is what you get, but it sure ain't what we need.

Walk it down. Talk it down. Sympathy. Luxury. Somebody will take you there. Walk it down. Talk it down. Sympathy. Luxury. Somebody will take you there.

95

BIG BLUE PLYMOUTH (Eyes Wide Open)

There is nothing that is stronger than the feeling that you get when your eyes are wide open. There is nothing like the feeling, you can never forget, when your eyes are wide open. Daytime was a feeling, but it's not over yet, are my eyes still open? We come a long long distance and we're never going back, got my eyes wide open.

I got both doors open. I got both doors open. I got the back door open. I got the screen door open.

In another time. In another place. There's a train running through. Right through the middle of the house.

Have I been dreaming, or have I been sick? Are my eyes wide open? Do I do it like that, or do I do it like this? Are my eyes wide open? Wearing out the carpet doing tricks with her hands, she's got her eyes wide open. Think about this, "Well I already have." I got my eyes wide open.

I got both doors open. I got both doors open. I got the back door open. I got the screen door open.

I don't understand. Oh, it's *not* just a sound. Oh, I don't understand. It doesn't matter at all.

See the little girl with her eyes rolled back in her head. She's got a complication, but she knows it'll work out fine. Naked as a baby, talking about the feeling she gets. In another time, in another place.

I got both doors open. I got both doors open. I got the back door open. I got the screen door open. I don't understand, it's just a sound. I don't understand. It doesn't matter at all.

STEPHEN LACK

ROAD TO NOWHERE

Well we know where we're going, but we don't know where we've been. And we know what we're knowing, but we can't say what we've seen. And we're not little children, and we know what we want. And the future is certain, give us time to work it out.

We're on a road to nowhere, come on inside. Taking that ride to nowhere, we'll take that ride.

I'm feeling okay this morning and you know, we're on the road to paradise. Here we go, here we go.

We're on a ride to nowhere, come on inside. Taking that ride to nowhere, we'll take that ride.

Maybe you wonder where you are, I don't care. Here is where time is on our side. Take you there . . . take you there.

We're on a road to nowhere. We're on a road to nowhere. We're on a road to nowhere.

There's a city in my mind, come along and take that ride and it's all right.

And it's very far away but it's growing day by day, and it's all right.

Would you like to come along? You can help me sing this song, and it's all right.

They can tell you what to do but they'll make a fool of you, and it's all right.

We're on a road to nowhere.

SU HUNTLEY/DONNA MUIR

Road to nowhere :

WITH OUR LOVE

It's just a look, and it makes the boys quiver. Yes, it's the look, and now they remember. Had they forgotten what this all means? I think they *want* to forget, and they hope that *this* time:

I won't look, I've got other things to do now. I forgot what it was, I've got to get to work now. And they say "Set an example for us" (I see it!). It can happen to me too.

And it didn't make any difference to us, but I forgot the trouble, *that's* the trouble. Forgot the trouble, *that's* the trouble. Forgot the trouble, *that's* the trouble. Forgot the trouble, that's the trouble with our love, with our love, with our love.

They hear words such as, "You're really special." (They can't face that feeling. They can't really tell.) I look out the window,

and I call that education. I see all
my friends standing out there.
And I call that education (sophis-
tication).

Had they forgotten what this all
means? Things come and go (and
I see them), and I won't be ne-
glected (not this time!).

MAKING FLIPPY FLOPPY

We are born without eyesight, we are born without sin, and our mama protects us from the cold and the rain. We're in no hurry, sugar and spice. We sing in the darkness, we open our eyes.

I can't believe it. People are strange. Our president's crazy, did you hear what he said? Business and pleasure, lie right to your face. Divide it in sections, and then give it away.

Well, there are no big secrets, don't believe what you read. We have great big bodies, we got great big heads. Run-a-run it all together. Check it out, still don't make no sense! Making flippy floppy, trying to do my best. Lock the door, we kill the beast. KILL IT.

Nothing can come between us. Nothing lets you down. Nothing strikes your fancy. Nothing turns you on. Somebody is waiting in the hallway. Somebody is falling down the stairs. Set someone free, break someone's heart. Stand up, help us out.

Everything is divided, nothing is complete. Everything looks impressive, do not be deceived. You don't have to wait for more instructions, *no one* makes a monkey out of me. We lie on our backs, feet in the air, rest and relaxation, rocket to my brain.

Snap into position, bounce till you ache. Step out of line and you'll end up in jail.

Bring me a doctor, I have a hole in my head. They are just people, and I'm not afraid.

Doctor! doctor! we have nothing in our pockets. We continue, but we have nothing left to offer. Faces pressed against the window. Hey! They are just my friends. Check this out, don't be so slick. Break our backs, it goes like this. . . .

STEWART WILSON

PERFECT WORLD

Words by David Byrne and Chris Frantz

Well, I know *what* it is, but I don't know *where* it is. Well, I know *where* it is, but I don't know what it looks like. Well, I know what it looks like, but I don't know where she comes from. Well, I know where she comes from, but I don't know what's her name.

And she said, "This is a perfect world. I'm riding on an incline. I'm staring in your face. You'll photograph mine."

And I've been walking, talking, believing the things that are true. And I've been finding the difference between right and wrong, bad and good. See me put things together, put them back where they belong. Am I just like the others? Have I always been singing the same song?

This is a perfect world. I'm riding on an incline. I'm staring in your face. You'll photograph mine.

Somebody said that it happens all over the world. I do believe that it's true. And the sun's coming up, and we're doing all the things that we should. Doesn't everybody here believe in the things that we do?

And she said, "This is a perfect world. I'm riding on an incline. I'm staring in your face. You'll photograph mine."

It's a strange situation. What's wrong with you? Baby! . . . baby! . . . baby! What're you doing in my house? And it's all true! There's nothing wrong with you!

And I said, "This is a perfect world. I'm riding on an incline. I'm staring in your face. You'll photograph mine."

EDDIE RUSCHA

I'VE BEEN WALKING, TALKING, BELIEVING

HEAVEN

Everyone is trying to get to the bar. The name of the bar, the bar is called Heaven. The band in Heaven plays my favorite song. They play it once again, they play it all night long.

Heaven is a place where nothing ever happens. Heaven is a place where nothing ever happens.

There is a party, everyone is there. Everyone will leave at exactly the same time. It's hard to imagine that nothing at all could be so exciting, could be so much fun.

Heaven is a place where nothing ever happens. Heaven is a place where nothing ever happens.

When this kiss is over it will start again. It will not be any different, it will be exactly the same. It's hard to imagine that nothing at all could be so exciting, could be so much fun.

Heaven is a place where nothing ever happens. Heaven is a place where nothing ever happens.

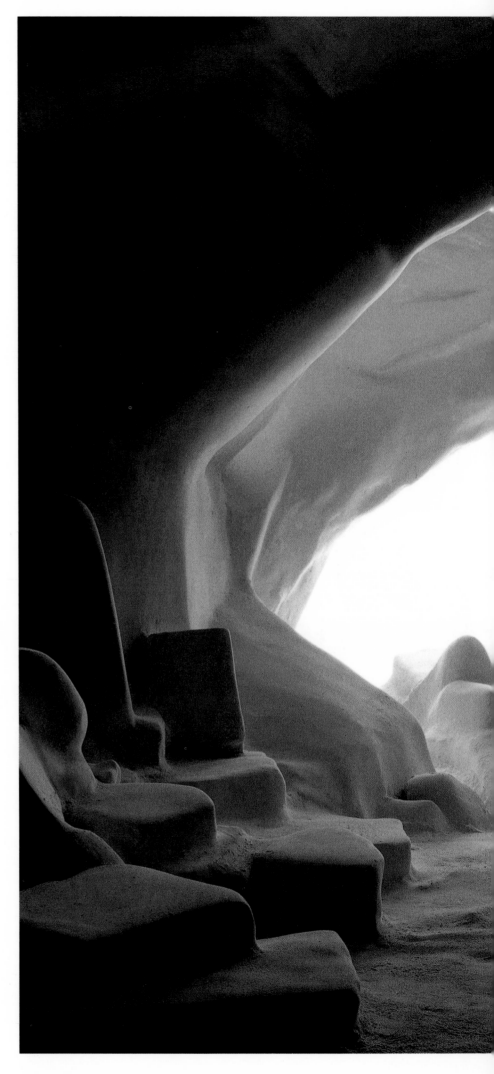

JAMES CASEBERE

PULL UP THE ROOTS

Hello again, yes indeed, my friend. I can tell, going get together again. I could be right, I could be wrong. I feel nice when I sing this song. And I don't mind, whatever happens is fine. Baby likes to keep on playing. What do I know? What do I know? Wilder than the place we live in. I'll take you there, I'll take you there. I don't mind some slight disorder. Pull up the roots, pull up the roots. And I know every living creature. Pull up the roots, pull up the roots.

I know you, I understand what you do. Yes, indeed, I put the hat on my head. Come out of your mess, bring yourself in. I feel nice when I start to sing. I can see, everyone else is like me.

Towns that disappeared completely. Pull up the roots, pull up the roots. Miles and miles of endless highway. Pull up the roots, pull up the roots. Colored lights and shiny curtains. I'll take you there, I'll take you there. Everything has been forgiven. Pull up the roots, pull up the roots.

Well I have a good time, when I go out of my mind. And it's a wonderful place, and I can't wait to be there. And I hear beautiful sounds coming out of the ground. Gonna take us a while but we'll go hundreds of times.

Baby likes to keep on playing. What do you know? What do you know? Wilder than the place we live in. I'll take you there, I'll take you there. And I don't mind some slight disorder. Pull up the roots, pull up the roots. And no more time for talking it over. Pull up the roots, pull up the roots.

Well I have a good time when I go out of my mind. And it's a wonderful place, and I can't wait to be there. I hear beautiful sounds coming out of the ground. Someone must have been high but I guess it's all right.

ANIMALS

I'm mad and that's a fact. I found out animals don't help. Animals think they're pretty smart. Shit on the ground, see in the dark.

They wander around like a crazy dog. Make a mistake in the parking lot. Always bumping into things. Always let you down down down down.

Animals think they understand. To trust in them is a big mistake. Animals want to change my life. I will ignore animals' advice.

They're never there when you need them. They never come when you call them. They're never there when you need them. They never come when you call them down down down down.

I know the animals are laughing at us. They don't even know what a joke is. I won't follow animals' advice. I don't care if they're laughing at us.

They're never there when you need them. They never come when you call them. They're never there when you need them. They never come when you call them down down down down.

They say they don't need money. They're living on nuts and berries. They say animals don't worry. You know animals are hairy! They think they know what's best. They're making a fool of us. They ought to be more careful. They're setting a bad example. They have untroubled lives. They think everything's nice. They like to laugh at people. They're setting a bad example. Go ahead, laugh at me.

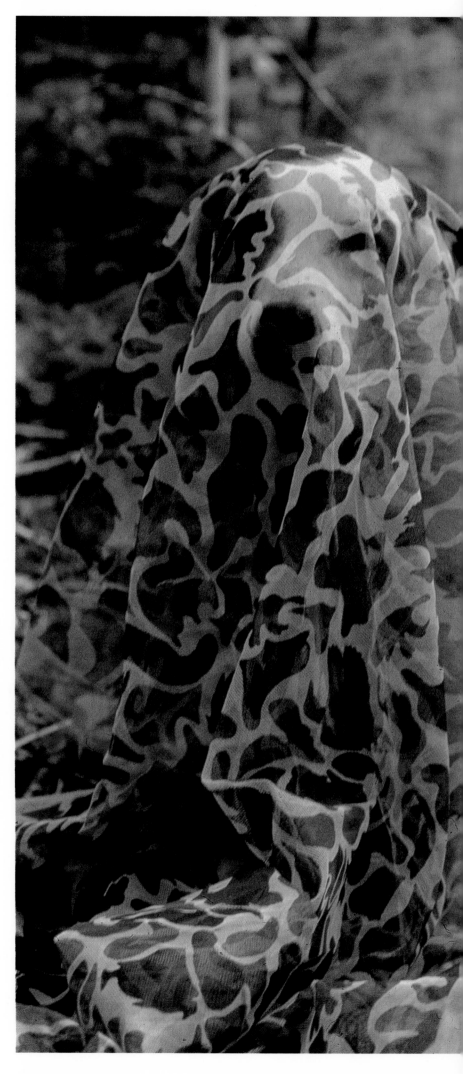

WILLIAM WEGMAN

THE GREAT CURVE

Sometimes the world has a load of questions. Seems like the world knows nothing at all. The world is near but it's out of reach. Some people touch it . . . but they can't hold on.

She is moving to describe the world. Night must fall now—darker, darker. She has messages for everyone. Night must fall now—darker, darker. She is moving by remote control. Night must fall now—darker, darker. Hands that move her are invisible. Night must fall now—darker, darker.

The world has a way of looking at people. Sometimes it seems that the world is wrong. She loves the world, and all the people in it. She shakes 'em up when she starts to walk.

She is only partly human being. Divine, to define, she is moving to define, so say so, so say so. She defines the possibilities. Divine, to define, she is moving to define, so say so, so say so. Holding on for an Eternity. Divine, to define, she is moving to define, so say so, so say so. Gone . . . ending without finishing. Divine, to define, she is moving to define, so say so, so say so.

The world moves on a woman's hips. The world moves and it swivels and bops. The world moves on a woman's hips. The world moves and it bounces and hops.

A world of light . . . she's gonna open our eyes up. A world of light . . . she's gonna open our eyes up. She's gonna hold it, move it, hoid it, move it, hold it, move it, hold it, move it. A world of light . . . she's gonna open our eyes up.

She is moving to describe the world. Night must fall now—darker, darker. She has messages for everyone. Night must fall now—darker, darker. She is moving by remote control. Night must fall now—darker, darker. Hands that move her are invisible. Night must fall now—darker, darker.

Divine, to define, she is moving to define, so say so, so say so. Night must fall now—darker, darker. She has got to move the world, to move the world, to move the world.

A world of light . . . she's gonna open our eyes up. A world of light . . . she's gonna open our eyes up. She's gonna hold it, move it, hold it, move it, hold it, move it, hold it, move it. A world of light . . . she's gonna open our eyes up.

Want to define . . . so say so, so say so. Divine, to define, she is moving to define, so say so, so say so. Night must fall now—darker, darker. She has got to move the world, to move the world, to move the world.

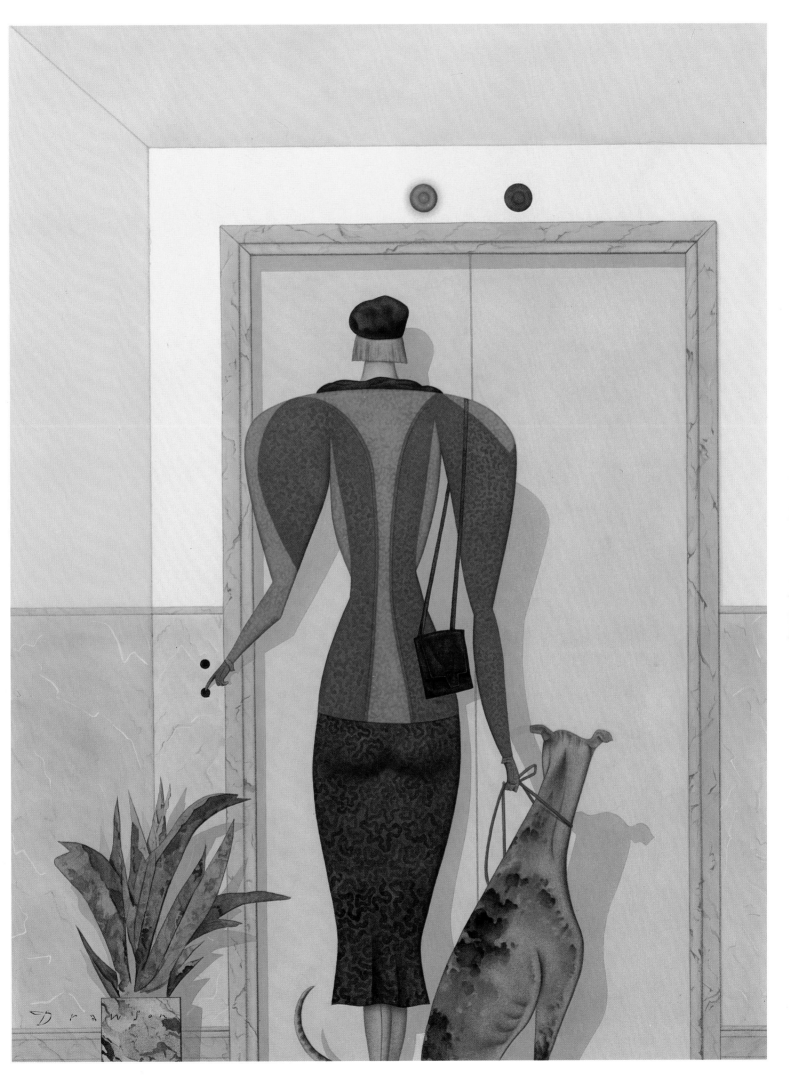

THE GIRLS WANT TO BE WITH THE GIRLS

The girls don't want to play like that, they just want to talk to the boys. They just want to do what is in their hearts, and the girls want to be with the girls.

And the boys say, "What do you mean?" And the boys say, "What do you mean?" Well there is just no love, when there's boys and girls. And the girls want to be with the girls. And the girls want to be with the girls.

Girls want things that make common sense, the best for all concerned. They don't want to have to go out of their way, and the girls want to be with the girls.

And the boys say, "What do you mean?" And the boys say, "What do you mean?" Well there is just no love, when there's boys and girls. And the girls want to be with the girls. And the girls want to be with the girls.

Girls are getting into abstract analysis, they want to make that intuitive leap. They are making plans that have far-reaching effects. And the girls want to be with the girls.

And the boys say, "What do you mean?" And the boys say, "What do you mean?" Well there is just no love, when there's boys and girls. And the girls want to be with the girls. And the girls want to be with the girls.

SARA SCHWARTZ

I GET WILD
(Gravity)
(Wild
Gravity)

Fooled around enough with numbers, let's not be ourselves today. Is it just my imagination? Is it just someone's face? Pleasantly out of proportion, it's hard to hold onto the ground. Now I didn't come to run, and this is everything. And gravity lets you down.

I get wild, wising up. I just can't let go. I get wild when I get ready, I can hardly talk. Living lights, special lights. Yellow turns to blue. I get wild, it's automatic. I can hardly move.

Go ahead and pull the curtains, check to see if I'm still here. Let me lose my perspective, something worth waiting for. Somewhere in South Carolina, where gravity don't mean a thing. And all around the world, each and everyone, playing with a heart of steel.

I get up, climbing out. How did I get home? I'll survive the situation, somebody shut the door. Beautiful, beautiful. Climbing up the wall. I get by on automatic. No surprise at all.

No one here can recognize you, here is everything that you like. Feelings without explanations, some things are hard to describe: the sound of a cigarette burning, a place there where everything spins. And the sound inside your mind is playing all the time, playing with a heart of steel.

I get wild, wising up. I just can't let go. I get wild . . . when I get ready, I can hardly talk. Red and white . . . black to gold. Yellow turns to blue. I get wild . . . it's automatic. I can hardly move.

I get up . . . pushing up. How did I get home? I'll survive the situation, somebody shut the door. Shut the door, shut the door. Climbing up the wall. I get by on automatic. No surprise at all.

JANET WOOLLEY

STAY HUNGRY

WORDS BY DAVID BYRNE
AND CHRIS FRANTZ

I think that we can signify our love now. Girl, you can initiate an impulse of love.

Stay hungry, stay hungry, stay hungry. Move a muscle, move a muscle, move a muscle. Make a motion, make a motion, make a motion. Pull it tighter, pull it tighter, pull it tighter. Double beating, double beating, double beating. Palpitation, palpitation, palpitation. Stay hungry, stay hungry, stay hungry.

Here's that rhythm again. Here's my shoulder blade. Here's the sound I made. Here's the picture I saved. Here I am.

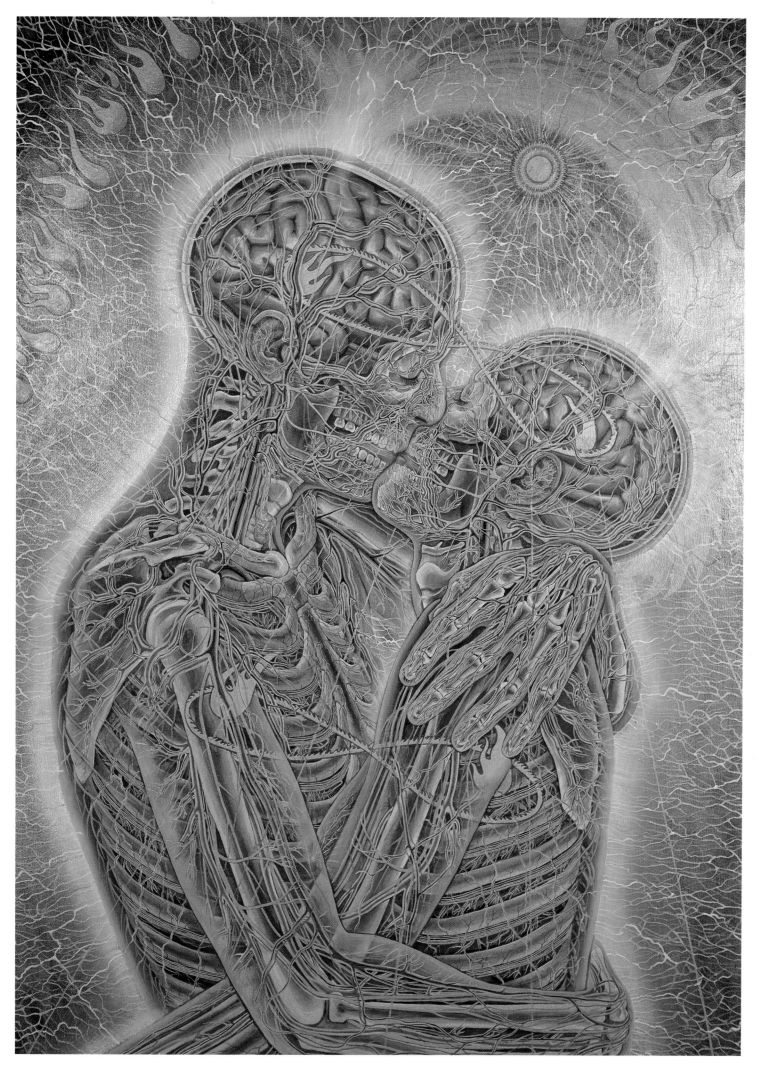

ALEX GREY

STAY UP LATE

Mommy had a little baby. There he is, fast asleep. He's just a little plaything. Why not wake him up?

Cute, cute, little baby. Little pee pee, little toes. Now he's coming to me. Crawl across the kitchen floor.

Baby, baby, please let me hold him. I wanna make him stay up all night.

Sister, sister, he's just a plaything. We wanna make him stay up all night, yeah we do.

See him drink from a bottle. See him eat from a plate. Cute, cute as a button. Don't you wanna make him stay up late?

We're having fun with no money. Little smile on his face. Don't you love the little baby? Don't you want to make him stay up late?

Baby, baby, please let me hold him. I wanna make him stay up all night.

Sister, sister, he's just a plaything. We wanna make him stay up all night, yes we do.

Sister, sister! (all night long). In the playpen! (all night long). Little baby goes ha! (all night long). I *know* you want to leave me. . . .

Why don't we pretend? There you go, little man. Cute, cute, why not? Late at night wake him up.

Baby, baby, please let me hold him. I wanna make him stay up all night.

Sister, sister, he's just a plaything. We wanna make him stay up all night.

Sister, sister! . . . woo! . . . (with the television on).

Little baby goes . . . wo! (all night long). Hey! Hey! Baby! (all night long). And he looks so cute (all night long). In his little red suit (all night long).

INDEX
OF
ARTISTS

(In alphabetical order)

Number(s) next to artists names indicate on which page(s) artwork is found.

Dimensions in inches: height × width × depth.

DUANE MICHALS 53
SEEN AND NOT SEEN, 1986
Photographic series of 6
Courtesy of the artist

RUSSELL MILLS 82–83
THE OVERLOAD
Small Silences Between, 1986
Mixed-media
31¼″ × 47″
Courtesy of the artist
Photo: David Buckland

VICTOR MOSCOSO 29
HOUSES IN MOTION, 1986
Cel-Vinyl paint on acetate over
airbrush background
11″ × 8¼″
Courtesy of the artist
© 1986 Victor Moscoso

JOSEPH NECHVATAL 86–87
I ZIMBRA
Maleficia, 1986
Projected drawing
Courtesy of Brooke Alexander,
Inc., N.Y.C.

JIM NUTT 60, 61
SLIPPERY PEOPLE
See For Yourself, 1986
Colored pencil on brown paper
11″ × 21″
Courtesy of the Phyllis Kind
Gallery, Chicago/New York

FRANK OLINSKY
12, 74–75
David Byrne, 1984
Ink and Pantone film
12″ × 9″
MOON ROCKS, 1986
Cut paper, ink, gouache and
collage
20″ × 20″
Courtesy of the artist

**FRANK OLINSKY AND
CAROLINE GREYSHOCK**
76–77
ARTISTS ONLY, 1986
Gouache on photograph
14″ × 17″
Photograph: Caroline Greyshock
Concept/painting: Frank Olinsky
Courtesy of the artists

NAM JUNE PAIK 66–67
TELEVISION MAN
T.V. Buddha, 1981–85
Video installation with sculpture
55″ × 115″ × 36″
The Rivendell Collection
Photo: James Dee

GARY PANTER 78–79
DRUGS, 1986
Acrylic on paper
22″ × 30″
Courtesy of the artist

ROBERT RAUSCHENBERG 15
Slingshot Lit #8
Light box assemblage with
lithography & screen print
84½″ × 54″ × 12″
Courtesy of the artist

EDDIE RUSCHA 104
PERFECT WORLD, 1986
*(Dedicated to the Sub-disco
Scene)*
Ink on paper
12″ × 8⅝″
Courtesy of the artist

EDWARD RUSCHA 105
PERFECT WORLD
Walking, Talking, Believing, 1986
Dry pigment on paper
50″ × 38″
Courtesy of the artist

SARA SCHWARTZ 114–115
*THE GIRLS WANT TO BE
WITH THE GIRLS*, 1985
Colored pencil
19″ × 20″
Courtesy of the artist

LAURIE SIMMONS 25
AND SHE WAS
Rooftops, 1984
Photograph
Courtesy of Metro Pictures,
N.Y.C.

GEORGE SNOW 39
CITIES
Iron Way of State, 1983
Collage
40″ × 30″
Courtesy of the artist

GEOFF SPEAR 34–35
*DON'T WORRY ABOUT THE
GOVERNMENT*, 1986
Photograph
Courtesy of the artist

JOOST SWARTE 68
FOUND A JOB, 1986
India ink and colored inks
9½″ × 7⅛″
Courtesy of the artist
© 1986 Jooste Swarte

JEFF TURTLETAUB 4, 5
AND DAVID BYRNE
Pool Polaroids, 1976
Red Polaroids, 1976
Polaroid Photos
Collection of David Byrne

ANNE TURYN 9
Untitled
(from *Illustrated Memories*)
Photograph
Courtesy of the photographer

BOYD WEBB 109
PULL UP THE ROOTS
Corpse, 1983
Photograph
Courtesy of Sonnabend Gallery,
N.Y.C.

WILLIAM WEGMAN 110–111
ANIMALS, 1986
Photograph
Courtesy of Holly Solomon
Gallery, N.Y.C.

WILLIAM T. WILEY 91
THE GOOD THING
*Michael Row the Botha Soul (No
More Up Art Hide)*, 1986
Watercolor
30⅛″ × 22¼″
Courtesy of the artist

STEWART WILSON 102–103
MAKING FLIPPY FLOPPY,
1986
Color xeroxes
2 Sheets: 14″ × 8½″
Courtesy of the artist

KRZSZTOF WODICZKO
36–37
IN THE FUTURE
Public projection at Grand Army
Plaza, Brooklyn, N.Y.
New Year's Eve
(Dec. 31, 1984—Jan. 1, 1985)
Organized by Prospect Park
Courtesy of Hal Bromm Gallery,
N.Y.C.

MARTIN WONG 40
*MY BIG HANDS
(FALL THROUGH THE CRACKS)*
Narcolepsy, 1986
72″ × 72″
Oil on canvas
Courtesy of Semaphore Gallery,
N.Y.C.

JANET WOOLLEY 117
I GET WILD (WILD GRAVITY),
1986
Acrylic and crayon
30″ × 20″
Courtesy of the artist

ROBERT YARBER 100–101
WITH OUR LOVE
Off, 1986
Oil and acrylic on canvas
72″ × 132″
Courtesy of Sonnabend Gallery,
N.Y.C.

TADANORI YOKOO 85
*BURNING DOWN THE
HOUSE*, 1986
Silkscreen and powder on canvas
40½″ × 28¾″
Courtesy of the artist

BOB HOPE? ZOELL 30–31
CREATURES OF LOVE
The End Is Near
Let's Get Married, 1986
Acrylic on canvas
72″ × 108″
Courtesy of the artist

ACKNOWLEDGMENTS

Special thanks to:

Susan Brand

David Byrne

Chris Frantz

Inge Hanson

Jerry Harrison

Elliot Hoffman

Laurie Kelliher

Gary Kurfirst

Lydia Link

Adelle Lutz

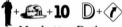

Manhattan Design

Craig Nelson

Overland

Edith Pavese

Andrea Starr

Tina Weymouth

—for their assistance and support.